Igneous Rocks

by Melissa Stewart

Heinemann Library
CHICAGO, ILLINOIS

© 2002 Reed Educational & Professional Publishing
Published by Heinemann Library,
an imprint of Reed Educational & Professional Publishing,
Chicago, Illinois
Customer Service 888-454-2279
Visit our website at www.heinemannlibrary.com

Designed by Ox and Company

An Editorial Directions book

Printed in China

06 05 04
10 9 8 7 6 5

Library of Congress Cataloging-in-Publication Data
Stewart, Melissa.
  Igneous rocks / Melissa Stewart.
    p. cm.—(Rocks and minerals)
Includes bibliographical references and index.
Summary: Provides an overview of igneous rocks including how they were formed,
their characteristics, where they are found, and uses throughout the world.
ISBN: 1-58810-256-4 (HC), 1-4034-0092-X (Pbk.)
  1. Rocks, igneous—Juvenile literature. [1. Rocks, Igneous. 2. Geology.] I. Title.
  QE461 .S745 2002
  552'.1—dc21   2001002757

Acknowledgments
The author and publishers are grateful to the following for permission to reproduce copyright material:

Photographs ©: Cover, Bob Daemmrich/The Image Works; p. 4, James P. Rowan; p. 5, R.W. Gerling/Visuals Unlimited, Inc.;
p. 7, Vince Streano/Corbis; p. 10 top, David Johnson/Reed Consumer Books, Ltd.; p. 10 bottom, A.J. Copley/Visuals
Unlimited, Inc.; p. 11, Lysbeth Corsi/Visuals Unlimited, Inc.; p. 12, Joe Carini/The Image Works; p. 13, Fritz Polking/Visuals
Unlimited, Inc.; p. 14, Adam Smith/FPG International; p. 15, James P. Rowan; p. 16, Dean Conger/Corbis; p. 17, Jeff
Greenberg/The Image Works; p. 18, Cameramann International, Ltd.; p. 19, Corbis; p. 20, Jack K. Clark/The Image Works;
p. 21, Gamma Liaison/Hulton Archive; p. 22, Grace Davies Photography; p. 23, James L. Amos/Corbis; p. 24, Dane S.
Johnson/Visuals Unlimited, Inc.; p. 25, Buddy Mays/Corbis; p. 26, Tess Young/Tom Stack & Associates; p. 27, Corbis; pp. 28,
29, Daemmrich/The Image Works.

Some words are shown in bold, **like this.** You can find out what they mean by looking in the glossary.

Contents

What Is a Rock?

This tombstone is made of granite. Granite is less expensive and easier to quarry than slate, another rock often used in tombstones many years ago.

What do Mount St. Helens in Washington and the sandy shores of Raasay, Scotland, have in common with a tombstone and some Native American tools? They are all made of igneous rock.

Igneous rock is one of three kinds of rocks found in the world. The other two kinds are **sedimentary rock** and **metamorphic rock.** Each kind of rock forms in a different way. Examples of igneous rock include granite, gabbro, basalt, obsidian, pumice, and tuff.

Rocks are all around you. They are under your feet and at the top of the highest mountains. They are in buildings and below raging rivers. Rocks come in all shapes and sizes. You can see tiny pebbles on the beach or along the side of the road. You can see giant boulders at a local park or in the woods.

All three kinds of rock are made of **minerals.** A mineral is a natural solid material. It always has the same chemical makeup and the same structure. This means that the **atoms** that mix together to form a mineral always arrange themselves in the same way.

SCIENCE IN ACTION

Petrologists—scientists who study rocks—can identify a rock by knowing where it came from and by looking at the **properties** of its minerals. For example, petrologists examine the color, the shininess, and the hardness of the minerals in a rock. They also study the size, shape, and arrangement of the crystals.

Most minerals have a **crystal** structure. Crystals usually have a regular shape and smooth, flat sides called **faces.**

Quartz is an example of a mineral sometimes found in igneous rock. The crystal structure of quartz is made up of silicon and oxygen atoms that are always arranged in the same way. A quartz crystal always has six faces.

Rhyolite is a light-colored igneous rock that contains some of the same minerals as granite. These rhyolite boulders lie in a riverbed in Mexico.

Layers of Earth

Earth is a giant ball of rock. The layer of rock that you walk on every day is called the **crust.** Below Earth's crust is a much thicker layer called the **mantle.** The mantle is made of hot, liquid rock called **magma.** Like oatmeal, magma is thick, but it can flow.

Earth's sizzling-hot **core** has two parts. The temperature of the melted metals that make up the outer core are at least 6,700 degrees Fahrenheit (3,700 degrees Celsius). The inner core is even hotter, but it is made of solid metals. The weight of all the overlying

Magma Movement

Inner Core (solid)

Outer Core (liquid)

Mantle

Crust

The thin, outer layer of Earth is the crust. The next layer, the mantle, is made of magma that is constantly moving. The core is made of an outer liquid core and an inner solid core.

DID YOU KNOW?

When Earth formed 4.6 billion years ago, the entire planet was made of molten magma. It took millions of years for Earth to cool enough for its crust to harden.

THAT'S INCREDIBLE!

You might wonder how scientists found out that Earth has three layers. After all, no one can travel to the center of our planet. It's much too hot.

Many years ago, seismologists—scientists who study earthquakes—noticed that waves of energy travel through Earth during, and just after, an earthquake. After carefully measuring the energy waves, seismologists realized that the waves speed up, slow down, and change direction as they zoom through the planet.

At first, scientists had trouble explaining these changes. Eventually, however, they decided that the movement of energy waves indicates that different parts of Earth's interior are made of different materials. In recent years, seismologists have studied earthquake waves to calculate how thick each layer is and to determine the makeup of each layer.

layers presses down on the inner core. All that pressure holds the **molecules** that make up the inner core so close together that they cannot turn into a liquid.

Just as heat from a mug of hot cocoa can transfer heat to your hands, Earth's core constantly releases heat to the cooler mantle. This flow of heat energy causes magma in Earth's mantle to slowly swirl in giant circles. As the hottest magma moves toward Earth's surface, cooler magma moves back down to take its place.

Land on the Move

Have you ever looked closely at an ice cube floating in a glass of water? Ice is less dense than liquid water, so a little bit of the ice always sticks above the water's surface. Earth's **crust** has a lot in common with the ice in a glass of water. The crust is broken into giant pieces called **plates.** Each plate floats on top of the **magma** in the **mantle.** The land and oceans are the part of the crust that always sticks above the magma.

As heat from Earth's **core** escapes and forces magma to move, Earth's plates move too. In some parts of the world, plates move apart, and long cracks called **rifts** are left behind. When rifts form under the ocean, the material from the mantle rises to the surface and creates new land on either

Earth's surface is broken into many plates. The major plates are labeled on this diagram. The plates are moving constantly, though very slowly, in the direction of the arrows. The Mid-Atlantic Ridge is a rift formed by two plates moving apart.

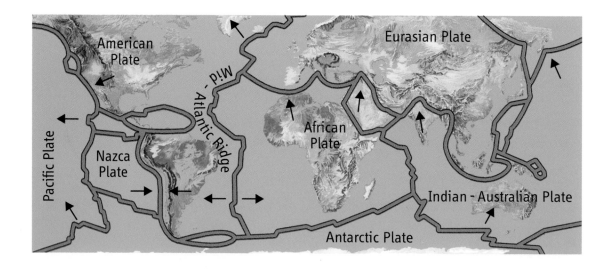

American Plate

Eurasian Plate

Mid - Atlantic Ridge

African Plate

Pacific Plate

Nazca Plate

Indian - Australian Plate

Antarctic Plate

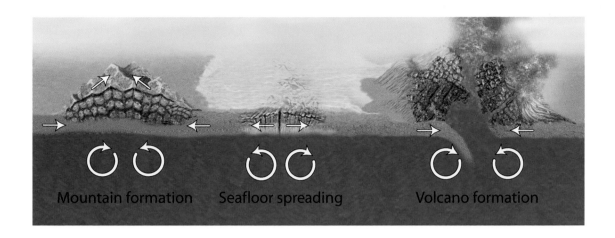

Mountain formation | Seafloor spreading | Volcano formation

side of the rift. This process is called **seafloor spreading.** As magma from inside Earth seeps through the Mid-Atlantic Ridge, it creates new seafloor. That is why North America and Europe are slowly moving apart, and the Atlantic Ocean is getting bigger.

In other parts of the world, plates bump into one another. Sometimes one plate slides over the other. Then the bottom plate moves down into the mantle where it melts. When two plates hit head-on and push against each other with great force, the land buckles and tall mountains form. When two plates scrape against each other, the result is a **transform fault,** such as the San Andreas Fault in California and the Dalkey Fault in Ireland. When enough pressure builds up along a fault, an earthquake occurs.

Mountains may form when two plates hit head-on. The seafloor expands as magma rises through a rift. When one plate moves below another, magma may rise to the surface and escape through a **volcano.**

WHAT A DISCOVERY!

In 1912, a German scientist named Alfred Wegner noticed that some of the continents seem to fit together like the pieces of a jigsaw puzzle. He suggested that Earth's crust is made of moving plates. Scientists couldn't imagine what would cause land to move, so they did not accept Wegner's theory. Now we know that Wegner was right. At one time, all the land on Earth formed a single continent called Pangaea.

Three Kinds of Rocks

Gabbro is one example of igneous rock. It is heavy and is usually a greenish color.

Sandstone is a sedimentary rock that forms as sand is pressed together over millions of years. Its color is determined by the material that binds the sand together.

Earth has three kinds of rocks—igneous, **sedimentary,** and **metamorphic.** Each kind of rock forms in a different way. Igneous rock forms when **magma** from Earth's **mantle** cools and hardens. Granite, basalt, pumice, rhyolite, andesite, and gabbro are all examples of igneous rocks.

Sedimentary rock forms as layers of mud, clay, sand, and other materials build up over time. The weight of the materials at the top of the pile presses down on the materials below. All that pressure cements the materials together to form rock. If you look closely at sedimentary rock, you may be able to see its layers. Limestone, sandstone, shale, breccia, and conglomerate are all examples of sedimentary rocks.

Metamorphic rock forms when heat or pressure changes the **minerals** that make up igneous rock, sedimentary rock, or another metamorphic rock. This often happens when Earth's **plates** collide and push up tall mountain ranges. As India crashes into the rest of Asia, the

THE MOST COMMON ROCK

Although sedimentary rock is the most common rock we see exposed on Earth's surface, most of our planet's crust is actually made of igneous rock. Many mountains are made of igneous rock. They form as lava spills out of the crust, cools, hardens, and slowly piles up. Igneous rock also covers the floors of all the oceans.

Himalaya Mountains—the tallest mountains on Earth—slowly rise into the sky. Millions of years ago, the Appalachian Mountains in North America and the Caledonian Mountains in Europe formed in the same way. Metamorphic rock also forms when a stream of magma bursts into the **crust** and cooks surrounding rock. Marble, slate, schist, gneiss, hornfels, and serpentinite are examples of metamorphic rock.

Schist is one of the toughest rocks on Earth. The pattern of minerals in this metamorphic rock resembles wood grain.

DID YOU KNOW?

The word "igneous" comes from a Latin term meaning "made from fire." Of course, igneous rock is not really made from fire, but Earth's inner heat does play an important role in moving the soft magma to places where it can cool and become solid igneous rock.

A Look at Volcanoes

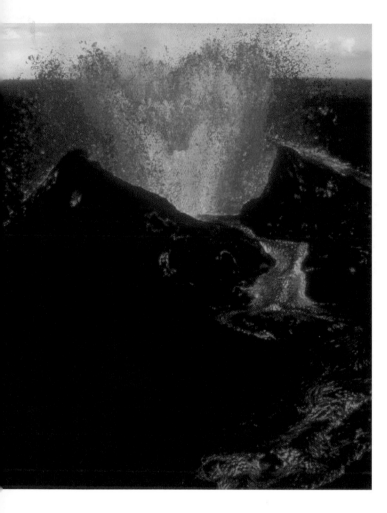

A **volcano** is a crack or hole in Earth's surface that extends through the **crust** and into the **mantle.** Some people also use the word volcano to describe the large mountain-like mound that builds up around the crack over time. Most volcanoes form in places where Earth's **plates** meet. So many volcanoes rise along the edges of the Pacific Plate that this area is sometimes called the "Ring of Fire."

Kilauea in Hawaii is the world's most active volcano. There is an observatory on the rim of its crater.

The lava that spews from volcanoes is **magma** that has escaped from Earth's mantle. When lava hits air or water, it starts to cool immediately. In a few days or weeks, the lava hardens and becomes igneous rock, such as basalt. If you look closely at some rocks, you can see their **crystals.** But the **minerals** that make up basalt cool so quickly that they have no time to form large crystals.

There are about 500 active volcanoes in the world today. When a volcano erupts, a gray cloud of ash fills the air, and lava flows out of the volcano. Scientists do not always know when a volcano will erupt or how much damage it will cause. In the past, volcanoes have destroyed entire towns and killed thousands of people.

The Hawaiian Islands are made of basalt, but there were no violent eruptions involved in their formation. These islands formed as lava slowly leaked out of a **hotspot**—a place where magma spikes through Earth's crust in the middle of a plate—and piled up over thousands of years. Eventually, the piles became tall enough to poke above the surface of the ocean and form islands.

Old Faithful, a **geyser** in Yellowstone National Park, is fueled by a hotspot. It erupts every thirty to ninety minutes, blasting steam and hot water up to 170 feet (50 meters) into the air.

THE FIVE DEADLIEST VOLCANOES IN HISTORY			
VOLCANO	NUMBER OF PEOPLE KILLED	LOCATION	DATE
Krakatau	36,000	Java, Indonesia	1883
Pelée	28,000	Martinique	1902
Nevado del Ruiz	23,000	Armero, Colombia	1985
Etna	20,000	Sicily	1669
Vesuvius	16,000	Pompeii, Italy	79

Cool as a Crystal

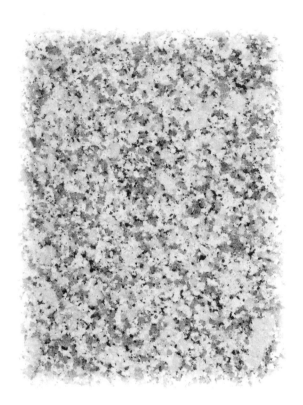

You can see the crystals of feldspar, mica, and quartz in granite. The red specks in this sample are made of feldspar.

DID YOU KNOW?

Gabbro and basalt are made of the same minerals—pyroxene, feldspar, and olivine. They look different because gabbro cools more slowly and, therefore, has much larger crystals.

If you look closely at pieces of granite or gabbro, you can see their **crystals.** That's because the material that formed these igneous rocks did not spill out of **volcanoes** and cool quickly. Instead, a pool of molten **magma** became trapped near the top of the **mantle** and cooled more slowly.

Most of the magma below Earth's surface circulates slowly through the mantle. Each time magma gets close to the **core,** it is reheated. However, when magma is caught near the surface, it eventually cools down and hardens to form igneous rock.

Even though the top of the mantle is much cooler than the bottom, it is still much warmer than the water or air at Earth's surface. As a result,

14

the **minerals** in igneous rock that forms below ground cool slowly over thousands of years. This gives the minerals time to form large, beautiful crystals.

Now that you know gabbro and granite form underground, you may wonder why we see them on the surface today. Over time, Earth's **plates** have moved, and rock that was once many miles below the surface is now exposed.

Mount Rushmore in South Dakota is made of granite, as are two huge, round boulders in Australia known as Devil's Marbles. These rocky structures formed deep underground and were later lifted above Earth's surface. Over time, wind and water have worn away at their surfaces.

A MOUNTAIN-SIZED MEMORIAL

Between 1927 and 1941, American sculptor Gutzon Borglum used dynamite to carve the faces of four great U.S. presidents on Mount Rushmore. Today the 60-foot (18-meter)-tall sculptures of George Washington, Thomas Jefferson, Theodore Roosevelt, and Abraham Lincoln can still be seen in the granite cliffs.

The Rock Cycle

Rocks are always changing. As **magma** cools to create new igneous rock, other kinds of rocks are being destroyed. You may think rock is indestructible, but over time, wind, water, and ice can be even tougher. Crashing ocean waves, raging rivers, whipping winds, and galloping glaciers can slowly wear away, or **erode,** even the hardest rock. Rocks can also be broken down when plant roots grow into cracks or crevices, when **acid rain** and snow fall, when they are repeatedly frozen and thawed, and when living creatures release chemicals from their bodies. These changes are called **weathering.** Have you ever seen a boulder that looked like it had mysteriously split in half? The split was probably the result of weathering.

DID YOU KNOW?

Half Dome Mountain (above) is a strangely shaped formation at Yosemite National Park in California. It is made of granodiorite—a kind of igneous rock. The softer layers of rock surrounding Half Dome were worn away as an ice-age glacier moved across the land. On average, a glacier travels about 650 feet (200 meters) a year, but some move much faster.

As rocks break down and wear away, the tiny pieces are picked up by rivers and streams. Eventually, these **sediments** travel all the way to the ocean. Over time, layers of sediments build up and form **sedimentary rock.**

As Earth's **plates** move, some of the sedimentary rock becomes part of the land. When the layers shift and compress, the sedimentary rock is exposed to tremendous heat and pressure. Over millions of years, the sedimentary rock may change into **metamorphic rock.** The rock may be pulled into the **mantle,** where it will melt and become magma. Eventually, some of that magma will cool to form igneous rock.

Melting to reform magma

Heat and pressure

Metamorphic Rock

Igneous Rock

Heat and pressure

Erosion and build up of sediment

Melting to reform magma

Erosion and build up of sediment

Sedimentary Rock

Melting to reform magma

Erosion and build up of sediment

The rock we see on Earth today has not always been here. Rock forms and breaks down in a never-ending cycle.

SEE FOR YOURSELF

The next time you visit the seashore or a large lake, pick up some pebbles along the beach. Compare them to pebbles you find in your yard or at a local park. The edges of the beach pebbles will be rounder and smoother than the land pebbles because water has worn them down. The beach pebbles show erosion at work.

Where on Earth Is Igneous Rock?

Sugar Loaf Mountain is one of the most famous landmarks in Rio de Janeiro, Brazil. It was exposed as wind and water eroded all of the softer rock around it.

DID YOU KNOW?

The oldest known rock in the world is located in western Australia. It consists of granite that is nearly four billion years old.

Igneous rocks are the most common rocks in Earth's **crust.** The seafloor is made of volcanic basalt. The Andes Mountains in South America are made of andesite. This volcanic mountain range has slowly risen as the Nazca **Plate** crashes into the American Plate. Black sand beaches in Hawaii, Scotland, New Zealand, and Greece are all made of tiny grains of igneous rock that came from **volcanoes.**

Some of the most incredible rock formations in the world are made of igneous rock that formed deep underground. Granite Tor in England and Sugar Loaf Mountain in Brazil formed when wind and water wore away all the surrounding rock.

There are many ancient legends that try to explain how Giant's Causeway in Northern Ireland formed. Today we know these steplike columns are made of basalt. As the rock is slowly **eroded** by the sea, it breaks into blocks that look like a huge staircase. Le Puy de Dôme in France is also made of igneous rock. It was once the central part of a volcano, but the surrounding rock slowly eroded over time.

Obsidian, a shiny volcanic igneous rock, is usually found in small amounts. However, giant rock formations known as the Glass Buttes in Oregon and the Valles Caldera in New Mexico are made entirely of obsidian.

DID YOU KNOW?

According to an ancient Native American legend, when a group of girls was chased by an angry bear, they ran as far as they could and then climbed up a rock where they hoped they would be safe. As the huge, ferocious bear jumped and clawed at its sides, the rock grew taller and taller to protect the girls. The rock, which Northern Plains tribes called Bear's Lodge, was considered a sacred site.

In 1906, President Theodore Roosevelt declared the 1,267-foot (386-meter)-tall basalt rock one of the nation's first national monuments. Located in Wyoming, it is now known as Devils Tower (right). Scientists believe that it is the core of an ancient volcano.

Igneous Rocks in Space

The Moon is made entirely of igneous rock. The highlands—the areas that look white from Earth—are made of anorthosite, norite, and troctolite. The Moon's dark patches, or marias, are made of basalt.

About ten billion years ago, a giant, spinning cloud of dust and hot gases began to form in our galaxy, the Milky Way. Eventually, a brightly glowing ball formed at the center of the cloud. That ball was our Sun. As more time passed, some of the remaining dust and gases began clumping together. As these larger objects hurtled through space, they collided with one another and slowly grew even bigger.

Eventually, a few very large objects formed. Close to the Sun, four small planets with rocky surfaces formed—Mercury, Venus, Earth, and Mars. As on Earth, the upper layers of the other rocky planets are made of igneous rock. Many moons, including Earth's Moon, are made entirely of igneous rock.

DID YOU KNOW?

Chondrites are the oldest known rocks in the solar system. These meteorites formed about 4.6 billion years ago. Chondrites are made of tiny, round igneous rocks called chondrules.

This incredible image of Asteroid 243 Ida was taken by the Hubble Space Telescope. It is 36 miles (58 kilometers) long and has many craters on its surface.

Farther out in the solar system, four gas giants formed—Jupiter, Saturn, Uranus, and Neptune. These planets do not have solid surfaces, but they are made of some of the same materials as the rocky planets.

Each year, about 19,000 bits of rock from other worlds strike Earth. Most of these **meteorites** are too small to notice. But sometimes scientists find football-sized meteorites on the ice in Antarctica. Then they can study the space rocks. Meteorites are often made of igneous rock. Many meteorites from Mars are made of pyroxenite. Some rocky chunks that have broken off from **asteroids** are made of pallasite.

UP CLOSE AND PERSONAL

In the late 1960s and 1970s, a dozen American astronauts visited the moon. Most of them had been trained as pilots, but Harrison "Jack" Schmitt was a geologist—a scientist who studies rocks and rock formations to try to understand how a moon or planet formed and how it has changed over time. During his *Apollo 17* mission, Schmitt observed the Moon's surface firsthand. Later, he described what he saw to other scientists.

How People Use Igneous Rock

The walls of the Empire State Building in New York City are made of granite. Granite is an important building material because it is very durable.

People use igneous rock in many ways. For example, most of the roads and parking lots in the United States are paved with crushed basalt because it is common and durable. Basalt is also used to build curbs. The most incredible structures ever built from basalt are the world-famous Moai statues at Anakena Beach on Easter Island. The giant structures, carved to look like human heads and upper bodies, were constructed by native people more than 400 years ago.

Granite is a very popular building material. Its strength and beauty make it a good choice for sculptures, tombstones, and buildings. The walls of the Empire State

Building in New York City are made of white granite. So are the towers at each end of Sydney Harbor Bridge in New South Wales, Australia. The Vietnam Veterans Memorial in Washington, D.C., is made of black granite. Gabbro and blue gray larvikite are also used as building materials. Like granite, they are widely available, strong, and beautiful.

Obsidian is a fast-cooling **volcanic** glass. It is usually pure black, but may also be brown or black with shiny bands of purple, green, and gold. Native American people used it to make tools and weapons, such as arrowheads. Because it has such tiny **crystals,** obsidian is hard and flakes easily. Other groups of early people used it to make masks, mirrors, and jewelry. Obsidian is also used to decorate stone buildings because it is pure black, shiny, and easy to shape.

Obsidian is an igneous rock. Because it is hard and chips easily, many native groups used it to make weapons.

Amazing Igneous Rocks

Have you ever found a little rock in the pocket of a new pair of jeans? That rock was probably pumice. Jeans are sometimes washed with pumice to give them a faded look. Pumice, an igneous rock, is the lightest rock on Earth. The holes you see in pumice are filled with air that was trapped when lava cooled quickly.

Pumice is so lightweight it can float in water. This igneous rock is an important ingredient in many household cleaners.

Pumice is not the only special igneous rock. Many people would like to find kimberlite. But they aren't as interested in the kimberlite as what may be nearby—diamonds and other valuable gems. Large, beautiful **crystals** often form in and around kimberlite as the rock slowly cools.

ODOR EATERS

A small company in Billings, Montana, is selling volcanic rocks from a local quarry as natural odor removers. No one knows exactly how they work, but they are popular. The company ships 30 tons a month to destinations throughout the United States, Mexico, Japan, Italy, and Taiwan. The rocks remove odors for two to four weeks and can be "recharged" by placing them in the sun for two days.

Pele's Hair is the name used to describe long, golden filaments of obsidian. These hairlike structures sometimes form when lava spurts from a **volcano,** is caught by the wind, and then cools in long, glassy strands before it hits the ground. If you saw Pele's Hair, you would probably never guess that it is a kind of rock.

When igneous rocks, such as rhyolite, basalt, or andesite, cool quickly, large gas bubbles may create holes inside them. As time passes, these cavities may fill with large quartz crystals, such as amethyst, or with beautifully banded agate. Craftspeople in ancient Greece and Rome often carved beautiful **cameos** from agate.

DID YOU KNOW?

Kimberlite is the most abundant rock at Crater of Diamonds State Park in Arkansas (above). If you visit the park, you can spend all day looking for diamonds and take home anything you find.

Is That an Igneous Rock?

Basalt is the most common kind of igneous rock. It may form six-sided columns when the rock cools and then fractures.

No matter where you live, you see dozens of rocks every day. They are in your house, in the walls of buildings, and on the ground. You've probably never paid too much attention to these rocks, but take a closer look. Some of them may be igneous rocks.

Knowing where a rock comes from can help you identify it. For example, if a rock came from a place where there was once—or still is—an active **volcano,** it is probably igneous rock—especially if it is smooth and glassy or hard and black. Sometimes lava spreads out in great sheets and covers very large areas of land. An area of Washington, Idaho, and Oregon called the Columbia Plateau is made of basalt that formed millions of years ago as a very large lava sheet cooled.

IMAGINE THAT!

Igneous rocks can tell a geologist where **magma** spilled onto the land thousands of years ago. For many years, scientists believed that the mountains in the Cascade Range in Washington were volcanic because they found many samples of igneous rock in the area. When one of the mountains, Mount St. Helens (left), erupted in 1980, researchers were not surprised.

To find out even more about a rock, you can study its **crystals.** Most rocks with medium or large crystals are igneous rocks that formed underground. Igneous rocks that formed as lava cooled have much smaller crystals.

A rock's color, texture, shininess, and hardness can also help you identify the **minerals** in it. In general, igneous rocks have a uniform texture and evenly distributed colors. Many igneous rocks contain minerals such as quartz, feldspar, olivine, pyroxene, biotite, mica, and sodalite. These minerals tend to be fairly hard.

Of course, one of the best ways to identify a rock is to study a field guide to rocks and minerals. These books show pictures of rocks and give detailed descriptions of them.

Be a Rock Hound

Now that you have learned how to identify igneous rocks, would you like to collect some? You can buy all kinds of beautiful and interesting igneous rock samples. You can also view them at a natural history museum, but it might be more fun to hunt for them in a local park, in a field, or in the woods.

These students are collecting rocks on a school field trip. Do you think the sample they are observing is made of igneous rock?

Before you begin planning your first rock hunting trip, you will need to gather a few pieces of equipment. You will also need to learn a few rules.

Once you have identified the rocks, you may want

DID YOU KNOW?

Rock and **mineral** clubs are very popular all over the world. These clubs sponsor exhibits, organize field trips, and may even help build museum collections. By joining a club, you can also meet other people who are interested in rocks.

to create a system for labeling, organizing, and storing them. Then you will always be able to find a specific sample later. You can arrange your specimens any way you like—by color, by **crystal** shape, by collection site, or even alphabetically. As your collection grows, being organized will become more and more important.

You can store your rock collection in a cardboard box. Be sure to label specimens.

WHAT YOU NEED

- Hiking boots
- A map and compass
- A pick and rock hammer to collect samples
- Safety glasses to keep rock chips out of your eyes
- A small paintbrush to remove dirt and extra rock chips from samples
- A camera to take photographs of rock formations
- A hand lens to get an up-close look at minerals
- A notebook for recording when and where you find each rock
- A field guide to rocks and minerals

WHAT YOU NEED TO KNOW

- Never go rock hunting alone. Go with a group that includes an adult.
- Know how to read a map and use a compass.
- Always get a landowner's permission before walking on private property. If you find interesting rocks, ask the owner if you may remove them.
- Before removing samples from public land, make sure rock collecting is allowed. Many natural rock formations are protected by law.
- Respect nature. Do not disturb living things, and do not litter.

Glossary

acid rain: rain that is polluted with acid in the atmosphere and that damages the environment

asteroid: chunk of rock that orbits the Sun within the solar system

atom: smallest unit of an element that has all of the properties of that element

cameo: small piece of jewelry that usually features a human head carved in relief

core: center of Earth. The inner core is solid, and the outer core is liquid.

crust: outer layer of Earth

crystal: repeating structural unit within most minerals

erode: to slowly wear away rock over time by the action of wind, water, or glaciers

face: smooth, flat side of a crystal

geyser: kind of hot spring that occasionally spews steam and hot water

hotspot: place in the middle of a plate where magma spikes through Earth's crust

magma: hot, soft rock that makes up Earth's mantle. When magma spills out onto Earth's surface, it is called lava.

mantle: layer of Earth between the crust and outer core. It is made of soft rock called magma.

metamorphic rock: kind of rock that forms when heat or pressure changes the minerals within igneous rock, sedimentary rock, or another metamorphic rock

meteorite: chunk of rock from space that hits Earth or another object in space

mineral: natural solid material with a specific chemical makeup and structure

molecule: smallest unit of a substance, made up of one or more atoms

plate: one of the large slabs of rock that make up Earth's crust

property: trait or characteristic that helps make identification possible

rift: crack in Earth's surface created when two plates move away from each other

seafloor spreading: process that occurs when Earth's plates move apart, creating a crack on the floor of the ocean

sediment: mud, clay, or bits of rock picked up by rivers and streams and dumped in the ocean

sedimentary rock: kind of rock formed as layers of mud, clay, and tiny rocks build up over time

transform fault: crack that forms on Earth's surface where two plates scrape against each other

volcano: crack in Earth's surface that extends into the mantle, and from which comes melted rock

weathering: breaking down of rock by plant roots or by repeated freezing and thawing

To Find Out More

BOOKS

Blobaum, Cindy. *Geology Rocks!: 50 Hands-On Activities to Explore the Earth.* Charlotte, VT: Williamson, 1999.

Christian, Peggy. *If You Find a Rock.* New York: Harcourt Brace, 2000.

Hiscock, Bruce. *The Big Rock.* New York: Aladdin, 1999.

Hopper, Merredith. *The Pebble in My Pocket : A History of Our Earth.* New York: Viking, 1994.

Kittinger, Jo S. *A Look at Rocks: From Coal to Kimberlite.* Danbury, CT: Franklin Watts, 1997.

Oldershaw, Cally. *3D-Eyewitness: Rocks and Minerals.* New York: Dorling Kindersley, 1999.

Pellant, Chris. *The Best Book of Fossils, Rocks, and Minerals.* New York: Kingfisher, 2000.

Ricciuti, Edward, and Margaret W. Carruthers. *National Audubon Society First Field Guide to Rocks and Minerals.* New York: Scholastic, 1998.

Staedter, Tracy. *Rocks and Minerals.* Pleasantville, NY: Reader's Digest, 1999.

ORGANIZATIONS

Geological Survey of Canada
601 Booth Street
Ottawa, Ontario
KIA 0E8
613/995-3084

U.S. Geological Survey (USGS)
507 National Center
12201 Sunrise Valley Drive
Reston, VA 22092
703/648-4748

Index